ALMOST IMPOSSIBLE

BRAIN BAFFLERS

TIM SOLE & ROD MARSHALL

Sterling Publishing Co., Inc.
New York

Mensa and the distinctive table logo are registered trademarks of
American Mensa, Ltd. (in the U.S.),
British Mensa, Ltd. (in the U.K.),
Australian Mensa, Inc. (in Australia),
and Mensa International Limited (in other countries)
and are used by permission.

Library of Congress Cataloging-in-Publication Data Available

2   4   6   8   10   9   7   5   3   1

Published by Sterling Publishing Co., Inc.
387 Park Avenue South, New York, NY 10016
© 2006 by Tim Sole and Rod Marshall
Distributed in Canada by Sterling Publishing
℅ Canadian Manda Group, 165 Dufferin Street
Toronto, Ontario, Canada M6K 3H6
Distributed in the United Kingdom by GMC Distribution Services
Castle Place, 166 High Street, Lewes, East Sussex, England BN7 1XU
Distributed in Australia by Capricorn Link (Australia) Pty. Ltd.
P.O. Box 704, Windsor, NSW 2756, Australia

Sterling ISBN-13: 978-1-4027-3274-4
ISBN-10: 1-4027-3274-0

Contents

Acknowledgments

Our thanks are due to many people, without whose help this book would not have been possible. To name but some:

The London Staple Inn Actuarial Society, which publishes *The Actuary* and which published its predecessor, *Fiasco*. Many of the puzzles in this book have been published in one of these magazines.

Roger Gilbert, former puzzle editor for the magazine *Actuary Australia*, and creator of some very fine puzzles.

The editors of *The Actuary*, *Fiasco*, and *Actuary Australia* for their support and encouragement to us as puzzle editors.

To those listed below (and we apologize if we have overlooked anyone) for creating, assisting with, or suggesting puzzles that we have used: 5–Pat O'Keefe, 8–David Kerr, 10–Alan Wilson, 21–Roger Gilbert and P.C. Wickens, 35–Alexander T. Brooks, 38–David Sole, 39–Chris Cole, 59–Roger Gilbert, 64–Tad Dunne, 66–Terry Wills, 68–Phil Watson and Kevin Kelly, 71–H.E. Dudeney, 81–Neil Parrack, 105–Henry Garfath, 107–Roger Gilbert, 116–Roger Gilbert, 117–Roger Gilbert.

Our respective wives, Judy Sole and Liz Marshall, without whose support this book would never have happened.

—Tim Sole and Rod Marshall

PUZZLES

1. It's easy to make an arithmetical expression equal to 24 from exactly three 8's $(8 + 8 + 8 = 24)$, but an expression for 24 can also be made from exactly three 1's, three 2's, and so on up to three 9's, using standard mathematical symbols: $+, -, \times, \div, \sqrt{}, !$ (factorial), decimal point, and $^-$ (repeating decimal). Using no more than three factorial signs in total, find such an expression for each digit from 1 to 9.

Answer, page 68

2. Donald has three daughters of whom he is exceedingly proud. All three are excellent logicians, and in his will he divides his properties among them.

He calls them together and tells them how many properties he owns and that each will inherit a different number of separate properties. He adds that the eldest will inherit the most properties (but not more than ten) and the youngest the fewest (with not less than one).

He then whispers in each daughter's ear how many properties she will inherit. After that, he proceeds from the eldest daughter to the youngest, asking each daughter if she can calculate how many properties each of her two sisters will inherit; each daughter replies "No" in turn. He does this a second time, and again all three reply "No." But then, when he asks the question a third time, the eldest daughter says, "Yes; each of the last two answers gave me some information, and I now know how many properties each of us will inherit."

How many properties will each daughter get?

Answer, page 76

3. Can you make a perfect square out of three matchsticks pointing in different directions, without bending or breaking them? (Some lateral thinking will be required!)

Answer, page 82

4. Insert the numbers from 2 to 10 in the nine small circles in such a way that the sum of the numbers appearing around each of the four large circles is the same.

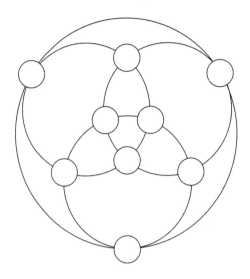

Answer, page 91

5. Hayley has a new sticker album with 250 gaps, each of which requires a particular sticker to fill it. The stickers to fill these gaps are sold individually in opaque sealed packets, so the contents of a packet are not known until the packet is purchased and opened.

Each packet costs 20 cents. But instead of buying every sticker individually, Hayley can write to the publisher of the album and request 25 specified stickers for $12.50, 50 for $25.00, 75 for $37.50, and so on.

Assuming there is an equal chance of a packet containing any of the 250 stickers, how many different individual stickers should Hayley collect before ordering one or more packs of 25 if she wants to minimize the expected cost of collecting a full set of stickers?

Answer, page 89

6. Two identical sets of dominoes, shown below, were used to make the robot on the opposite page. The dominoes in one set were all placed vertically, while the dominoes in the other set were all placed horizontally. The dominoes may, of course, be rotated from the positions shown. Identify the position of each domino in the robot.

Horizontally placed dominoes:

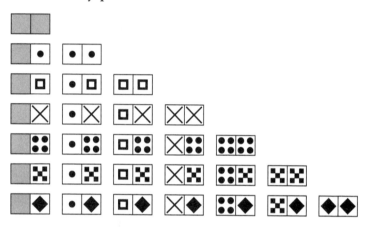

Vertically placed dominoes:

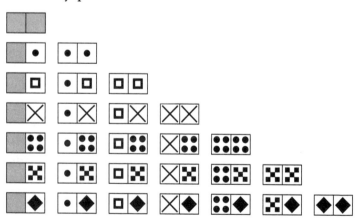

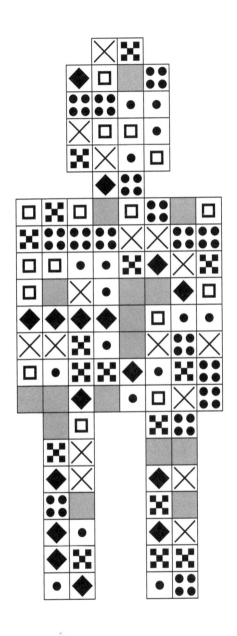

Answer, page 78

7. In this long division problem, all but two of the digits have been replaced with a blank. Can you supply the missing numbers?

$$
\begin{array}{r}
\_\_8\_\_ \\
\_\_\,)\overline{_____} \\
\underline{\_\_\_} \\
\_\_ \\
\underline{\_\_} \\
\_\_\_ \\
\underline{\_\_\_} \\
2
\end{array}
$$

Answer, page 71

8. Dozing in the classroom, Sarah awoke to hear her teacher ask, "Sarah, what comes next in this series?" Sarah looked at the blackboard and saw the following:

1, 2, 4, 5, 7, 8 ...

With no time to think, Sarah guessed:

11, 12, 13, 14, 15, 16 ...

After a pause, the teacher congratulated Sarah and moved on to a new topic. Sarah was very relieved, but when the class received its homework, the first question was:

1, 2, 4, 5, 7, 8, 11, 12, 13, 14, 15, 16, ?, ?, ?, ?

What are the next four items in the series?

Answer, page 73

9. Walking down the street, you overhear one person saying to another:

**"There is too much space between rose
and and and and and and crown."**

How should the sentence be punctuated, and what jobs from the list below might the two people have had?

Architect	Gardener	Moneylender	Taxi driver
Botanist	Historian	News vendor	Undertaker
Courier	Innkeeper	Orthodontist	Veterinarian
Dentist	Jeweler	Plumber	Waiter
Engineer	Karate teacher	Radiologist	Yacht maker
Firefighter	Lawyer	Sign painter	Zoologist

Answer, page 63

10. The local kindergarten is thinking of making posters that show all the different ways of adding together two or more integers from 1 to 9 to make 10. For instance: $1 + 9 = 10, 9 + 1 = 10, 2 + 8 = 10, 8 + 2 = 10$, and $2 + 1 + 2 + 1 + 1 + 2 + 1 = 10$. (Sums that contain the same numbers but in a different order are considered to be different.)

The kindergarten has wall space for ten large posters, and there will be space on each poster for up to 50 possible solutions. Is that enough space for the kindergarten to display every possible solution?

Answer, page 61

11. There are three jugs with capacities of 11, 13, and 17 cups. Each jug contains 9 cups of water. By pouring from jug to jug (and not spilling any water), how can you measure exactly 8 cups of water?

Answer, page 69

12. What word, expression, or name is depicted below?

Answer, page 87

13. While playing unattended one day, Thomas decided to build larger cubes out of a box of individual sugar cubes. So, emptying out the box onto the floor and using the sugar cubes as if they were building blocks, Thomas made three larger, solid cubes, with no sugar cubes left over.

At this point the family dog bounded into the room and sent the sugar cubes flying in all directions. The dog then picked up one of the sugar cubes in his mouth and left, crunching noisily.

Knowing he would be blamed for the mess if he didn't clean it up, Thomas picked up the remaining sugar cubes. Once he had done this, however, the temptation to keep playing with them proved too strong, and he began building again. This time he built two cubes rather than three, and again no sugar cubes were left over.

What is the smallest number of sugar cubes that could have been in the box when Thomas started playing with them?

Answer, page 84

14. You're probably familiar with puzzles like "12 = M. in a Y." where the goal is to identify the original phrase (12 = months in a year). The puzzle below is similar, but you are asked to provide the numbers as well. On the first line, for instance, 1,001 (Arabian Nights) – 1,000 (words that a picture is worth) = 1 (wheels on a unicycle).

A.N.	– W. that a P. is W.	= W. on a U.
A.M.	– F. on a P. of G.	= S. to E.S.
D. in F. in a L.Y.	– Y. of M. in a S.A.	= S. in a D. of C.
G. in a H.T.	+ R. on the O.F.	= L. on a S.
N. on a D.	– Q. in a G.	= O. in a P.
H. on a G.C.	+ D. in a F.	= D.F. at which W.F.
D. in a R.A.	– L. of the A.	= S. on a C.

Hint: the numbers on the right form a series.

Answer, page 67

15. A circular road is 31 miles long. There are six gas stations on the road, and it so happens that for every distance from 1 mile, 2 miles, 3 miles, and so on up to 30 miles, there are two gas stations which are that distance apart from each other on the road.

The simplified map below (not to scale) shows the two stations that are one mile apart. Can you determine the positions of the other four gas stations?

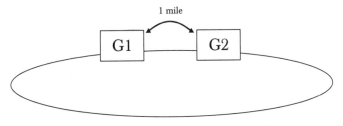

Answer, page 91

16. Each clue in the crossword below takes the form of a number. This number is equal to the product of the values of the letters in the corresponding word, where the value of a letter is equal to its position in the alphabet; thus A = 1, B = 2, C = 3, D = 4, and so on up to Z = 26. The clue for, say, RARE would therefore be $18 \times 1 \times 18 \times 5 = 1{,}620$.

ACROSS				DOWN			
1	1,536	**17**	14,040	**1**	17,100	**14**	810
4	257,040	**19**	420	**2**	80	**16**	1,725
7	3,675	**21**	23,400	**3**	9,800	**17**	42,768
8	720	**22**	831,600	**4**	101,250	**18**	14,820
10	8,820	**24**	145,800	**5**	5,292	**19**	32,400
12	7,560	**26**	300	**6**	519,840	**20**	2,160
13	151,200	**27**	1,436,400	**9**	2,268,000	**23**	1,400
15	228,000	**28**	6,825	**11**	567,000	**25**	1,350

Answer, page 75

17. After leaving the shopping mall, a shopper decided to walk home. (Her home is somewhere on the map below, but is not shown.) She wanted to take as short a route as possible, and she knew she could set off in either direction to achieve this. So she tossed a coin to determine which way she would go.

MALL

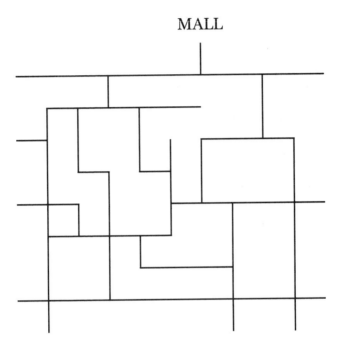

After completing more than half her journey, she reached the intersection where her favorite cafe is situated, and popped in for a coffee. When she left the cafe, it was once again the case that she could set off in either of two directions and still travel the shortest distance to complete her journey home.

Where is the cafe, and where does the shopper live?

Answer, page 81

18. The square of 567 is 321,489, and these two numbers contain each of the digits from 1 to 9 once and once only between them. What other three-digit number and its square have this property?

Answer, page 77

19. A hexagonal plot of land contains six houses as shown below. The six homeowners have agreed that they would like to erect fences to subdivide the whole plot into equal plots for each of them, with each house naturally being on its own plot of land. One of the homeowners pointed out that this could be done by dividing the plot into six congruent (but irregular) pentagons. Where would the fences have to be erected to achieve this?

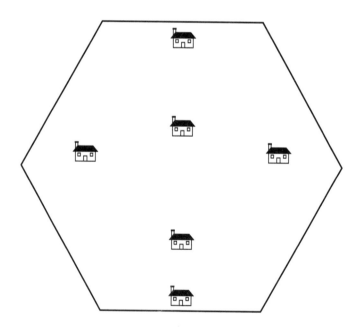

Answer, page 79

20. What is the smallest number that leaves a remainder of 1 when divided by 2, a remainder of 2 when divided by 3, a remainder of 3 when divided by 4, and so on up to a remainder of 17 when divided by 18?

Answer, page 93

21. Without using a calculator or computer, can you find two integers whose squares add up to exactly 100,000?

Once you've done that, do the same for 1,419,857, given that the only prime factor for this number is 17.

Answer, page 69

22. All the digits in the following multiplication problem have been replaced with letters. (A letter always represents the same digit throughout the problem.) Can you reconstruct the original multiplication?

TWO × TWO = THREE

Answer, page 72

23. A number of identical planes, each of which has a tank that will hold just enough fuel to travel exactly halfway around the world, are all based on a small island. If the planes can only refuel from the island or from another plane of their fleet, what is the smallest number of planes that would be required for one plane to complete a great circle around the world, with each plane involved in the maneuver returning safely to the island? Assume that planes can refuel and transfer fuel instantaneously, and that all planes travel at the same constant speed.

Answer, page 85

24. When Rachel looked at the board displaying the hymn numbers of the three carols to be sung at the Christmas Eve service, she was struck by the following:

- Each of the digits from 1 to 9 appeared on the board.
- Each number was a three-digit prime.

Given that the sum of the carols' numbers was less than 1,000, what were the numbers of the carols?

Answer, page 63

25. The set of whole numbers has been split into two groups according to a particular rule; the first ten numbers in each group are shown below.

1	4
2	5
3	9
6	11
7	12
8	13
10	14
15	18
16	19
17	20

The number 100 is also in the second group. In which group does 1,000,000 belong?

Answer, page 65

26. Which four-digit number is equal to its first digit to the power of its second digit, multiplied by its third digit to the power of its fourth digit?

Answer, page 88

27. Two men share the plot of land that their houses are built on. They have agreed to divide the land equally (with each owning the piece of land that his house is built on), but are not sure how best to divide the rest. Since they know you're a puzzle expert, they turn to you.

The diagram below shows the area in question, with the two houses marked in black. Where should the dividing fence be erected so that the two pieces of land *excluding* the houses are equal in area and have the same shape? (Rotations and reflections of a shape are considered to be equivalent.)

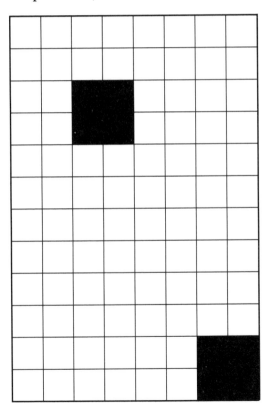

Answer, page 67

28. A pilot wants to begin his plane's descent at point D, but he is told by air traffic control to maintain his altitude and fly directly north. After six minutes of flying, the plane is directly above the control tower (point C). The pilot is then told to fly northwest for three minutes before turning at point T and heading back the 30 miles to point D.

This holding pattern is repeated a few times until the pilot is instead instructed to turn 90 degrees to the left upon arriving at point D. 30 miles later (at point B), the plane is directed back to the point directly above the control tower. Assuming that the plane has a constant speed throughout and that the time lost in turning is immaterial, how long does it take the plane to fly from point B to point C?

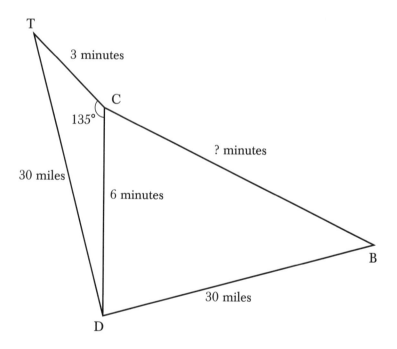

Answer, page 70

29. Find the triangle with the shortest perimeter where:

a) The sides are of different integral lengths.
b) The area is a perfect square.

To determine the area of the triangle, use Hero's formula (shown below); let the lengths of the sides be a, b, and c, and let s be half the perimeter, or $\frac{1}{2}(a + b + c)$:

$$\text{Area of triangle} = \sqrt{[s(s - a)(s - b)(s - c)]}$$

Answer, page 79

30. There is a well-known person whose name, when entered into the first and fourth rows of the diagram below, will spell four-letter words in all six columns. Who is it?

O	B	O	G	I	A
A	O	V	O	R	W

Answer, page 62

31. Choose a two-digit number and multiply its digits together. If the answer you get is another two-digit number, repeat the process of multiplying the digits together until you end up with a single digit. (For example, choosing 48 would require two multiplications, giving you the chain 48 → 32 → 6.) Are there any two-digit numbers that require more than three multiplications to reach a single digit?

Answer, page 72

32. A single set of dominoes has been used to make the "big W" below. However, two halves of two dominoes have been replaced with question marks. The disguised symbols are the black diamond and the single black dot, but not necessarily in that order. Identify the position of each domino.

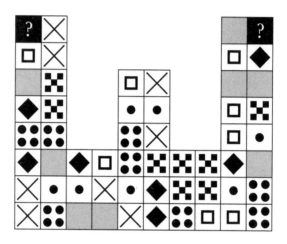

The set of dominoes:

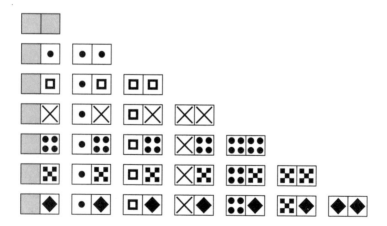

Answer, page 75

33. This puzzle is harder than it looks (and it doesn't look that easy). Find angle BEC.

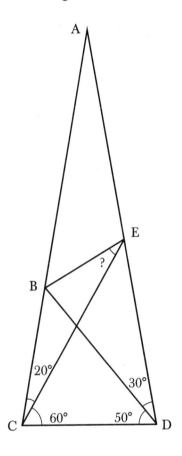

Answer, page 80

34. Take an 8-by-8 chessboard and remove the upper left and bottom right square. Can 31 dominoes, each rectangular and measuring 1-by-2, be placed to cover the chessboard's remaining 62 squares?

Answer, page 79

35. David inherited a rectangular 12-acre plot of land from a great-uncle who lived in the country. Since David prefers the city to the country, he decides to lease out part of the property, but cannot decide how best to subdivide the rectangle or how big the piece he retains should be.

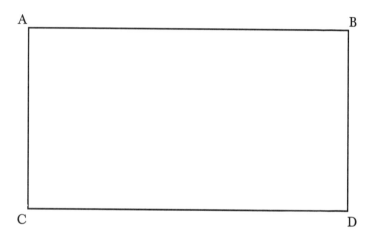

He mentions this to a friend, who offers to divide the property so that it can be broken up into plots of exactly one acre, two acres, three acres, and so on up to twelve acres, to allow David the maximum flexibility in subleasing the land. David is concerned at the cost of doing this, but his friend assures him that it can be done by erecting just two straight fences (which may if necessary cross one another), assuming that adjacent fenced-off plots may be combined when leasing out part of the property.

Where did the friend, who did not know the measurements of the plot of land, suggest the two fences be built?

Answer, page 83

36. A king (who weighs 156 pounds), queen (84 pounds) and prince (72 pounds) are stuck at the top of a tower. A pulley is fixed to the top of the tower, and running over the pulley is a rope with a basket at each end. One basket has a removable 60-pound weight in it. The baskets are only big enough to hold two people or one person and the weight. There are no restrictions on operating the pulley with the baskets empty or with just the weight, but for safety's sake there cannot be more than a 12-pound difference in weight between the two baskets if anyone is in either basket.

How do all three royals escape from the tower?

Answer, page 90

37. What word, expression, or name is depicted below?

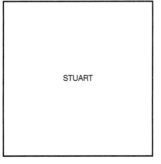

Answer, page 69

38. Arrange the letters below into a 3-by-3 grid to spell six words (three reading across and three reading down).

A   E   E   E   H   O   R   S   T

Answer, page 77

39. Sixteen tiles, eight black and eight white, have been arranged in a 4-by-4 square as shown. A tile can be moved by picking it up, placing it outside the array at either end of the row or column that it came from, and then closing the gap by sliding that tile (and any tiles between it and the empty space) into the gap to restore the square array.

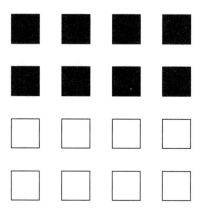

It's easy to find a way of achieving a checkerboard pattern in just eight moves if all the moves are made vertically. Can you find a way to make such a pattern by alternating vertical and horizontal moves?

Answer, page 73

40. A soccer ball consists of a valve, an inner skin, and 32 leather pieces sewn together to make its outer skin. Twenty of these leather pieces are regular hexagons with edges of unit length, and the other twelve are regular pentagons, also with edges of unit length.

If it takes five inches of thread to sew together two unit-length edges of leather, how much thread will be needed to sew the outside skin of the soccer ball?

Answer, page 78

41. What three letters should be placed in the three empty circles so that the longest possible word (which may be more than eight letters long) can be spelled out by reading around the circles? You may start from any circle and read clockwise or counterclockwise.

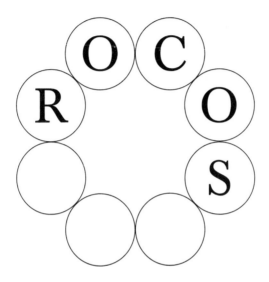

Answer, page 87

42. What type of music is missing below?

     __   **N**   **B**   **Q**   **K**   __   **N**   **R**

Answer, page 61

43. A traveler in the desert is heading for a camp twelve miles to the north. Five miles to the east of him a road runs in a straight line to the camp. He can travel twice as fast on the road as in the desert. What route should he take to reach the camp in the shortest time?

Answer, page 92

44. You are given four bags of coins; each bag contains thirteen coins. Two of the bags contain genuine coins only, and the other two bags contain counterfeit coins only.

You know the exact weight of a genuine coin, and you also know that counterfeit coins, in comparison to genuine coins, may be one or two grams underweight or overweight.

Counterfeit coins within one bag are all identical to each other, but may or may not be identical to the coins in the other counterfeit bag. How can you identify the two bags of counterfeit coins with a single weighing on a postal scale? (You may take as many coins from as many bags as you like.)

Answer, page 64

45. Three snooker players were presented with an unusual challenge. From a stock of three red and two yellow balls, three balls were chosen at random and each was then concealed in a different box. The challenge was for each player in turn to look inside two of the boxes to see if they could determine the color of the ball in the other box.

The first player looked inside boxes 1 and 3, but was not able to determine the color of the ball in box 2. The second player, having watched player one, then looked inside boxes 2 and 3, but could not then determine the color of the ball in box 1. Having watched players one and two, the third player then stated the color of the ball in one of the boxes, without even bothering to look inside the other two.

Which box did she name, and what was the color of the ball in it?

Answer, page 71

46. A right triangle measuring $5 \times 12 \times 13$ has an area (in square units) equal to its perimeter (in units). Name another right triangle with integral measurements that has this property.

Answer, page 77

47. Each of the four boxes below represents a different word or phrase, and the words/phrases have a common theme. What are the four words or phrases and what is the theme?

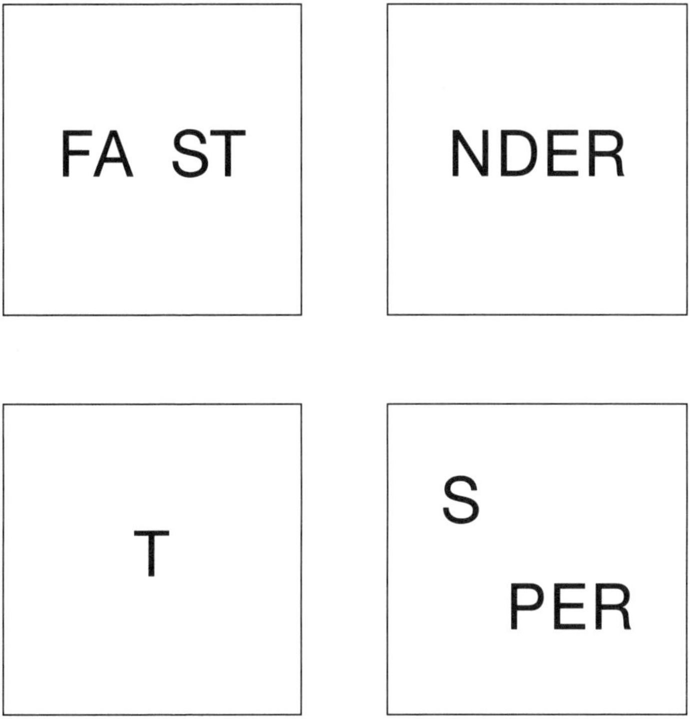

FA ST

NDER

T

S
PER

Answer, page 88

48. Ten identical squares have been arranged to form the letter E, as shown below:

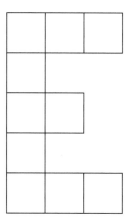

a) Cut the E into five pieces that can then be rearranged to form one large square without flipping over any of the pieces. (Rotating them is allowed, however.)

b) Cut the E into *four* pieces that can then be rearranged to form one large square. This time you are allowed to flip pieces over as well as rotate them.

Answer, page 72

49. In a certain code, the following pairs of words are equal:

acne = made   ahoy = robe   van = bun
fable = flay   pave = ply   beer = yeah

Using this code, what word does "khaki" equal?

Answer, page 81

50. Six people sit down to play a game of Clue, then realize that the board has been mislaid. Undeterred, they agree that each player will simply take turns making a suggestion (or, in due course, an accusation), and that any room can be chosen each time.

A quick refresher on the rules: One character, weapon, and room card are set aside; the rest of the cards are dealt out (with six players, this means everyone will receive three cards). When a suggestion is made, the next player must disprove it if he can; if he holds no cards that match part of the suggestion, the next player must disprove it if he can, and so on.

You are player A, and deal yourself Miss Scarlet, the Revolver, and the Ballroom. The game then progresses with the following suggestions (DB means "disproved by"):

Player	Character	Weapon	Room	DB
B	Col. Mustard	Dagger	Billard Room	E
C	Prof. Plum	Lead Pipe	Study	E
D	Mrs. White	Wrench	Conservatory	F
E	Mr. Green	Wrench	Library	F
F	Mrs. Peacock	Revolver	Hall	A
A	Mr. Green	Candlestick	Dining Room	F
B	Mrs. Peacock	Rope	Ballroom	E
C	Col. Mustard	Wrench	Lounge	B
D	Prof. Plum	Dagger	Kitchen	B
E	Prof. Plum	Lead Pipe	Study	B
F	Mrs. White	Lead Pipe	Conservatory	E

Player F disproved your suggestion of Mr. Green with the Candlestick in the Dining Room by showing you the Dining Room. Now make the winning accusation.

Answer, page 89

51. Wanda wants to mail a trombone that's 54 inches long at its shortest, but the post office limits parcel sizes to a maximum of 48 inches in length. What can she do?

Answer, page 93

52. Five men are stranded on a desert island whose only other resident is a single monkey. The only food on the island is coconuts. The five men collect all the coconuts they can find, and promise to divide them equally.

The night after they finish collecting the coconuts, the first man (fearing his companions are untrustworthy) decides to take his share while the other castaways are asleep. On dividing the coconuts into five equal piles, he finds there is one coconut left over, so he gives it to the monkey. He then hides his share and puts the rest of the coconuts back into one big pile and goes to sleep.

The second man, unaware that he had been beaten to the punch, then does the same thing. That is, he divides the coconuts into five equal piles, finds one left over that he gives to the monkey, hides what he thinks is his share, and puts the rest back into one big pile. After he goes to sleep, the third, fourth, and fifth men surreptitiously repeat the exercise. So, in all, there were five secret trips that night, and five coconuts for the monkey.

When the sun rose it was obvious to all that many of the coconuts were missing, but, as each man was guilty, none of them said anything about it. Instead, they peacefully divided the remaining coconuts equally, leaving one coconut left over which—you guessed it—they gave to the monkey.

What is the smallest number of coconuts that the fifth man could have ended up with?

Answer, page 75

53. What property having to do with fourth powers do the three numbers below have in common?

1,634   8,208   9,474

Answer, page 82

54. Samantha, a treasure hunter, found the following message:

> *From Secret Place to Crossbones Rock*
> *Pace out what steps you may.*
> *Turn right at rock and pace the same*
> *And you'll have found Point A.*
>
> *Return to Secret Place and count*
> *Your steps to Hangman's Tree.*
> *Turn left at tree and now count down*
> *To take you to point B.*
>
> *Halfway between points A and B*
> *You'll find my treasure case,*
> *But what a shame that you can't know*
> *About my Secret Place.*

She knows where Crossbones Rock and Hangman's Tree are located, but unfortunately does not know the whereabouts of Secret Place. Can you help her find the buried treasure?

Answer, page 68

55. Find a number between 100,000 and 1,000,000 which is a perfect square and which has its digits in strictly ascending order.

Answer, page 70

56. Four matches are placed on a table to make a square. Without moving these matches or placing any match on top of another, add four more matches to make three squares in total.

Answer, page 88

57. Here's one for mathematicians. What is the next term in this series?

10   22   36   55   122   220   ?

Answer, page 79

58. How can the five pieces shown below be rearranged (without overlapping) to form a single square?

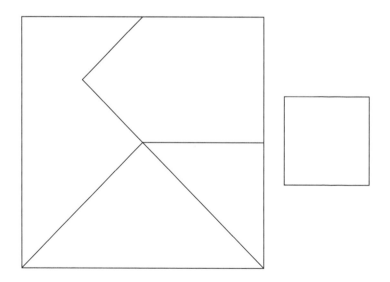

Answer, page 62

59. Andy has several pairs of blue socks and several pairs of gray socks. He keeps them all mixed up in a bag. He tells his aunt what socks he has, and says that if he pulls out two socks at random, there is a 50 percent chance that they will be a matching pair.

Andy's aunt thinks he needs more socks, so she buys him 24 more pairs (some blue, some gray). That's a lot of socks, but Andy's aunt tells him that if he puts these new socks in his bag with the rest, he will still have a 50 percent chance of pulling out a matching pair.

How many socks does Andy now have?

Answer, page 84

60. How many squares are there on a chessboard? (The answer is not 64!)

Answer, page 81

61. Five inventors need to cross a river with their five inventions (one per inventor), using a rowboat that will carry up to three people or inventions in any combination.

The inventors are very secretive about their inventions and each will not allow their invention to be in the presence of another inventor unless they are present too. All of the inventors can row, as can just one of the inventions, which is a robot. The robot, as well as being able to row, can also load and offload itself and any other inventions from the boat.

Before each crossing begins, the boat must be fully emptied before the ship is loaded up again. How can the five inventors cross the river with their inventions, using just the rowboat?

Answer, page 86

62. Here's another puzzle where, given an abbreviated phrase which corresponds to a number (M. in a Y.), the goal is to identify the original phrase (12 = months in a year). Unlike puzzle 14 on page 13, though, here all the abbreviations on a line are equal to each other. On the first line, for instance, 2 (nickels in a dime) = 2 (pints in a quart) = 2 (dice used to play Monopoly).

N. in a D.	=	P. in a Q.	=	D.U. to P.M.
S. in a Y.	=	S. on a S.	=	F. on M.R.
F. in a F.	=	P. on a P.T.	=	C. in S. of an A.
A. on an O.	=	K.H. of E.	=	P. in a G.
P. in a B.A.	=	Y. in a D.	=	L.I.
I. in a F.	=	S. of the Z.	=	D. of C.

Hint: the numbers form a series.

Answer, page 77

63. A five-digit security code is such that in each of the following numbers, one and only one of the digits is in the same position as the security code.

06582	58064
19086	67123
24937	71657
32023	81459
45900	96880

So we can tell from looking at 06582, the first number on the list, that 00000 and 28560 are possible security codes, but 11111 (which has no matches with 06582) and 06999 (which has two matches) are not. What is the security code?

Answer, page 84

64. Near the end of a party, everyone shakes hands with everybody else. Vanessa then arrives and shakes hands with only those people she knows, which is not everyone at the party. By doing this, she increases the total number of handshakes by 25 percent. How many people did Vanessa know?

Answer, page 64

65. Each of the four boxes below represents a different word or phrase, and the words/phrases have a common theme. What are the four words or phrases and what is the theme?

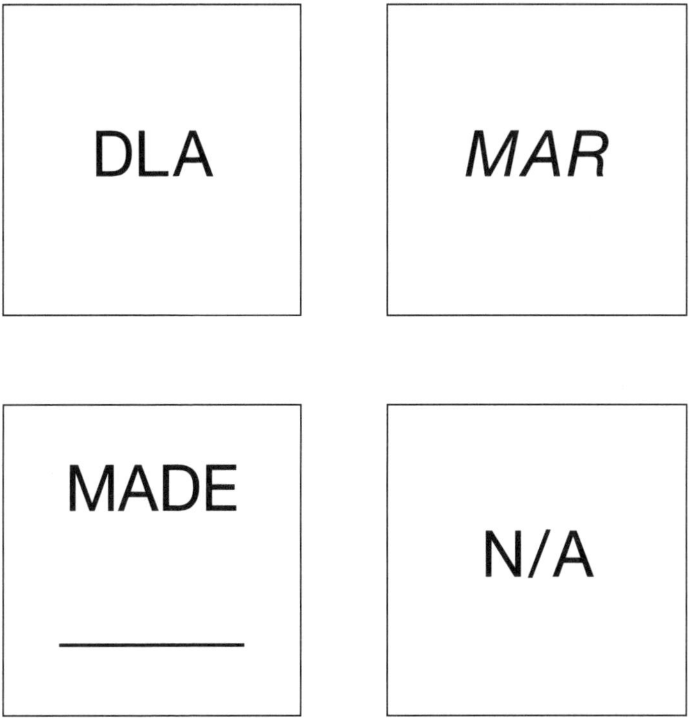

DLA	*MAR*

MADE ———	N/A

Answer, page 72

66. In the diagram below, each of the digits from 1 to 7 inclusive appears exactly eight times. Furthermore, the digits in the eight cells marked with a caret are all the same as each other, as are the digits in the eight cells marked with an asterisk. The sum and product of the digits in each row and column is indicated. Can you reconstruct the grid?

C1	C2	C3	C4	C5	C6	C7	Row totals
		^					Sum: 32 Product: 24,192
*	*						Sum: 26 Product: 2,800
							Sum: 13 Product: 7
^	^	*		^	^		Sum: 26 Product: 5,670
				*	*		Sum: 26 Product: 2,800
							Sum: 43 Product: 326,592
^	^	^		*			Sum: 27 Product: 7,560
				*	*		Sum: 31 Product: 22,400
Sum: 27 Product: 4,320	Sum: 32 Product: 25,920	Sum: 28 Product: 8,640	Sum: 56 Product: 5,764,801	Sum: 19 Product: 384	Sum: 32 Product: 13,500	Sum: 30 Product: 14,400	

Once you've done that, give yourself a brief pat on the back and then take a deep breath: the puzzle's not finished quite yet! You see, the diagram was originally constructed from the 28 domino pieces shown on the top of the next page:

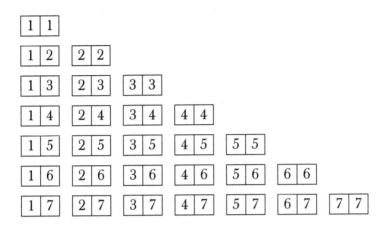

To complete the puzzle, reconstruct the original grid by placing all the dominoes in the correct location.

Answer, page 61

67. A Pythagorean triangle has an area of 666,666. No side of this triangle shares a common factor with another side or is smaller than 666. What is the length of the triangle's hypotenuse?

Answer, page 91

68. In 1998, the U.K. Institute of Actuaries celebrated its 150th anniversary. At that time, a puzzle was proposed that asked for each of the integers from 1 to 150 to be made using only the digits 1, 9, 9, and 8; parentheses as required; and the standard mathematical symbols: $+, -, \times, \div, \sqrt{}$, ! (factorial), decimal point, and $^{-}$ (repeating decimal).

The number that eluded most would-be solvers was 148. It isn't easy to find, but there is a solution for this number as well. What is it?

Answer, page 88

69. An orienteer climbs two hills, A and B, and on the top of each measures the angle between a familiar landmark and the top of the other hill. Having done this, she notices that one angle is twice the other. Checking her map, she then sees that A and B are five miles apart, and that the distances between the hilltops and the landmark are four and six miles as shown:

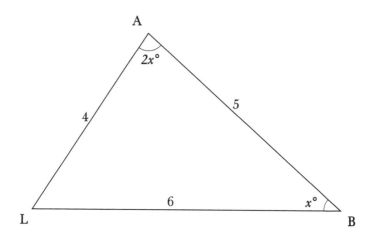

Prove geometrically that she has not made a mistake in her measurements.

Answer, page 66

70. A teacher wrote the number 139,257 on the blackboard and asked the class to write the number in base 8. One student noticed that the answer, 417,771, is three times the first number if both numbers are considered to be in base 10.

What are the lowest and highest numbers (in base 10) to have this property?

Answer, page 63

71. Tom, Dick, and Harry met for a picnic. Tom brought 15 items, Dick brought 9 items, and Harry brought 8 coins of equal value to be shared by the other two as a reimbursement for bringing food for him to share.

Assuming the men consumed equal shares of food (and all the items are of equal value), how should the money be divided?

Answer, page 68

72. What is the smallest right triangle that will completely fit inside another right triangle for which:

- The larger triangle has a side that is shorter than all three of the smaller triangle's sides.
- All six sides are integral.

Answer, page 84

73. There is a well-known person whose name, when entered into the second and fourth rows of the diagram below, will spell five-letter words in all seven columns. Who is it?

C	A	W	C	C	S	A
B	R	O	T	A	D	E
E	M	G	H	S	Y	D

Answer, page 73

74. Using the digits 1 to 9 in ascending order, a standard arithmetical sign between each pair of digits, and parentheses as required, find an alternative expression to the one below that still equals 100.

$$1 + 2 + 3 + 4 + 5 + 6 + 7 + (8 \times 9) = 100$$

Answer, page 78

75. In the game of bridge, hands are commonly assessed by assigning points to the high cards using the system below, and then adding up the points:

- 4 points for an ace
- 3 points for a king
- 2 points for a queen
- 1 point for a jack

Can you find a distribution of cards in which a partnership can make a grand slam against any defense, but with the partnership having the smallest possible number of points?

Answer, page 63

76. A 3-by-3-by-3 magic cube is a cube made of 27 smaller cubes (numbered from 1 to 27) where all the rows, columns, pillars, and main diagonals (the ones that pass through the center of the cube) have a common sum.

Is it possible to find such a 3-by-3-by-3 magic cube where the central cube is numbered 14? What about a 3-by-3-by-3 magic cube where the central cube is *not* numbered 14?

Answer, page 85

77. The diagram below shows an arrangement of the ten digits from 0 to 9 in ten circles, where the sums formed by adding the numbers in each pair of adjacent circles are all different.

If you rearrange the ten digits in the circles, what is the smallest number of different sums for adjacent circles that can be achieved?

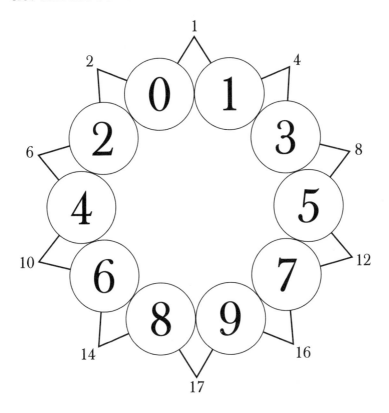

Answer, page 87

78. Can you rearrange the seven letters in the phrase NEW DOOR to spell one word?

Answer, page 70

79. The number 120 has the property that the sum of its divisors (1, 2, 3, 4, 5, 6, 8, 10, 12, 15, 20, 24, 30, 40, 60, and 120) is equal to three times the original number. What other three-digit number has divisors that sum to exactly three times the original number?

Answer, page 88

80. In the expression below, each letter represents a different digit from 1 to 9.

$$\frac{A}{DE} \; + \; \frac{B}{FG} \; + \; \frac{C}{HI} \; = \; 1$$

What are the three fractions?

Answer, page 75

81. Using the digits 1, 2, 3, 4, and 5 exactly once each in each expression, parentheses, decimal points (but not repeating decimals), and the standard arithmetical symbols +, −, ×, and ÷, find expressions equal to 111, 222, 333, 444, 555, 666, 777, 888, and 999.

Answer, page 62

82. Almost all whole numbers can be expressed as the sum of no more than eight positive cubes. For example, the number 121 needs only six:

$$121 = 4^3 + 3^3 + 3^3 + 1^3 + 1^3 + 1^3$$

Remarkably, there are just two exceptions to this rule. The first is 23, which needs nine positive cubes $(2^3 + 2^3 + 1^3 + 1^3 + 1^3 + 1^3 + 1^3 + 1^3 + 1^3)$, and the second is 239, which also needs nine positive cubes, but which can be solved in two different ways. What are they?

Answer, page 78

83. A set of dominoes, plus one extra double (a duplicate of one of the double dominoes in the set), was used to make the shape below. The symbol on the extra double also appears in the upper left and upper right corners of the shape, but has been replaced with question marks. Can you identify the position of each domino?

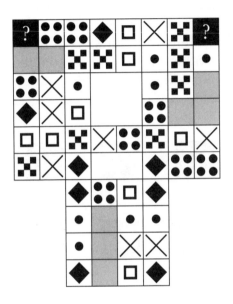

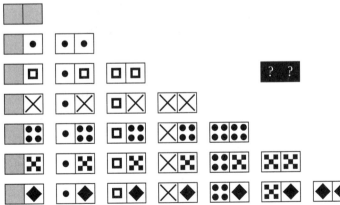

Answer, page 65

84. Fill in the empty squares in the grid below according to the following rules:

- Each square must contain one of the digits from 1 to 7.
- In each of the four rows and four columns, each of the digits from 1 to 7 must appear exactly once.
- Each of the white numbers already contained within the grid must equal the sum of the eight digits surrounding it.

Answer, page 90

85. Here's another one for mathematicians. What is the next term in this series?

2   12   36   80   150   ?

Answer, page 69

86. What word, expression, or name is depicted below?

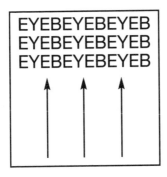

Answer, page 73

87. Which word is the odd one out?

laughing	**canopy**	**stupid**
understudy	**hijack**	**burst**

Answer, page 87

88. The military base of a fighting unit has four missiles to protect it from attack by air. The missiles are placed 50 miles north, 50 miles east, 50 miles south, and 50 miles west of the military base. Each missile has a range of 70 miles and is designed to harmlessly self-destruct if it does not hit its target before reaching the end of its range.

During a training exercise in which each missile was pointing to the next missile clockwise around the base, the four missiles were accidentally and simultaneously fired, sending them on a spiral route centered on the base. If the missiles collide above the base, then the base will be destroyed. Will the missiles get that far, or will the base survive?

Answer, page 67

89. Without using trial and error, find the number n and the digit d in the following equation:

$$[3 \times (300 + n)]^2 = 898,d04$$

Answer, page 93

90. An astronaut, hoping to discover life on the moon, laid a trip wire around the moon's equator that was just two inches clear of the surface. He didn't catch anything, so he decided to raise the wire to six inches above the surface. The moon has a diameter of 2,160 miles. How much extra wire will he need? (Assume the moon is perfectly spherical.)

Answer, page 79

91. A car is parked on a steep hill when the brakes suddenly fail. In the first second, the car rolls 12 inches. How far will it have rolled after five seconds?

Answer, page 66

92. In the multiplication problem below, each of the digits from 0 to 9 occurs exactly twice.

$$
\begin{array}{r}
- \, - \, - \\
\times \quad \underline{- \, - \, -} \\
- \, - \, - \\
- \, - \, - \\
\underline{- \, - \, -} \\
- \, - \, - \, - \, -
\end{array}
$$

Can you reconstruct the problem?

Answer, page 65

93. Find a 10-digit number where the last 10 digits of its square equal the original 10-digit number. An example using three digits is 376, the square of which is 141,376.

Answer, page 70

94. Just by guessing (and using some inspiration!), can you find the square root of this number?

12,345,678,987,654,321

Answer, page 75

95. Each empty square in the grid below is to be filled with a single letter. When read consecutively (inserting spaces where appropriate), the 18 letters spell out a well-known object.

The numbers in the grid represent the difference in value between adjacent letters, when each letter is given a numerical value equal to its position in the alphabet (that is, A = 1, B = 2, C = 3, and so on up to Z = 26). So, the digit 4 in the grid could separate the letters A and E, B and F, C and G, and so on. What is the object?

	7		4		13		5		5	
5	■	15	■	14	■	9	■	4	■	4
	13		5		8		18		13	
8	■	14	■	1	■	14	■	14	■	17
	9		10		7		10		18	

Answer, page 72

96. Without rotating any of the 16 pieces in the square below, rearrange them to make another square with common eight-letter names reading across each row.

Hint: The names alternate between male and female.

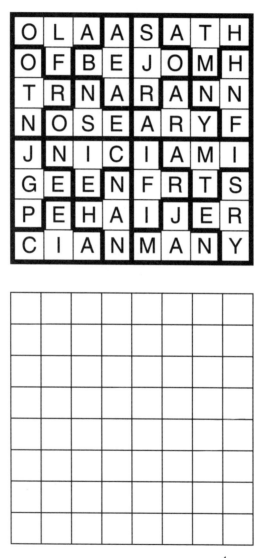

Answer, page 88

97. I'm thinking of four positive integers that are different from each other, and that total less than 18. If I told you both their product and the smallest of the four number, you'd be able to identify all four numbers. But you don't know their product and you don't know the smallest number . . . or do you?

Answer, page 82

98. Is it true that the capital of Norway is in Czechoslovakia?

Answer, page 91

99. If TED^3 = VINDICATE, and different letters represent different digits, is it DAVE or VIC that is two times IAN?

Answer, page 63

100. The name of a famous 20th-century world leader is depicted below. Who is it?

Answer, page 89

101. Would it be easier for a helicopter to take off from the surface of the moon or the surface of the earth?

Answer, page 77

102. What is the next term in this series?

A   E   F   H   I   K   ?

Answer, page 60

103. The diagram below shows two circuits. The top circuit contains two 1-ohm resistors in series and has a resistance of 2 ohms. The bottom circuit contains two 1-ohm resistors in parallel and has a resistance of 0.5 ohms.

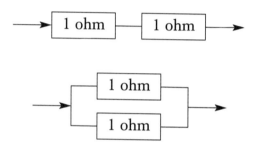

The circuit below is also composed of 1-ohm resistors. What is the resistance of the circuit?

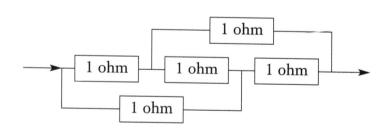

Answer, page 73

104. The variables *a*, *b*, and *c* represent three different nonzero digits. Find their values, given that the three-digit number $abc = b^c - a$.

Answer, page 93

105. Garfath Crescent is a semicircle whose diameter is an exact number of yards and less than a mile (1,760 yards). Along its straight side runs a hedge, and on its curved side stand 26 trees. (The diagram does not show their placement to scale.)

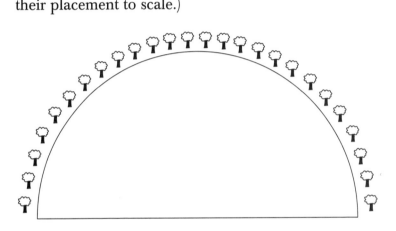

The distance from the center of any tree to either end of the hedge is a nonzero, integral number of yards. How long is the hedge?

Answer, page 68

106. An incomplete 10-digit code (using all the digits from 0 to 9) is shown below. It's an easy code to remember, as it is based on a particular well-known pattern. Are the two digits in the middle 17 or 71?

8 5 4 9 ? ? 6 3 2 0

Answer, page 79

107. A man-made pond has a flat base and vertical sides. In the center of the pond, a statue is to be erected using three identical concrete cubes (placed side by side) as the statue's foundation.

When the first concrete cube is placed flat on the bottom of the pond, the water level rises three inches. When the second and third concrete cubes are placed flat on the bottom of the pond, the water level rises four inches on both occasions. How big are the cubes?

Answer, page 74

108. What word, expression, or name is depicted below?

Answer, page 63

109. A man decreed in his will that $240,000 should be divided equally among his grandchildren—but only those who were monks or nuns at the time of his death. When he died, the monks received the same total amount as the nuns, and each of the grandchildren who benefited from his bequest received $56,000 more than they would have if all of the man's grandchildren had shared the money equally.

How many grandchildren did the man have when he died?

Answer, page 71

110. The winner of a game show is offered a choice of three envelopes, one of which contains a check for a million dollars while the other two contain small gift certificates. The contestant knows the contents of the envelopes, but doesn't know which one contains the grand prize.

Once the contestant has chosen an envelope, the game show host (who does know the contents of each envelope) then opens one of the remaining two envelopes to reveal a gift certificate, as he always does. He then asks the contestant if he wants to keep the envelope he has already chosen or swap it for the remaining unopened one.

What should the contestant do, and what is his chance of winning the grand prize?

Answer, page 65

111. Wht s th lwst whl nmbr tht wld nt b dscrbd nql f t wr wrttn n th sm stl s ths qstn?

Answer, page 88

112. The finals of the Tiddlywinks Club Championship features two players: Tiddle and Wink. Both players know that in any one game between them, Tiddle's chance of winning is two in three.

The championship is a best-of-nine series. Tiddle says that, according to the odds, after six games the score should be 4–2 to him, but to save time, he'd be willing to start the championship from a base score of 3–2 in his favor, thereby leaving Wink a chance of being tied 3–3 after game six.

Wink would like to give himself the best chance of winning the championship. Should he accept Tiddle's offer?

Answer, page 86

113. Susie swims at a constant speed. The distance from the jetty to where her boat is moored would normally take Susie ten minutes to swim. However, because she has the current with her, she is able to swim from the jetty to her boat in exactly five minutes. How long will it take her to swim back?

Answer, page 81

114. I bought four items from my local convenience store. The bill came to $7.11. I thought that amount must have been wrong, as I had seen the cashier multiplying the four prices together instead of adding them. (The cash register was broken, so he had to use a calculator instead.)

When I questioned the cashier about it, he agreed that he had multiplied the prices together, but said that in this case it didn't matter since the sum of the four items was also $7.11.

What were the prices of the four items?

Answer, page 84

115. What piece of equipment used more in New York than in Florida is depicted below?

Answer, page 67

116. A triangular farm is divided into four paddocks by fences that run in straight lines from two of the corners as shown below:

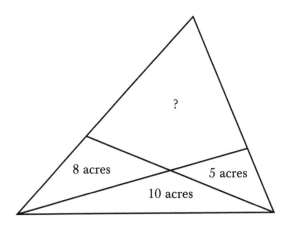

The areas of the three triangular paddocks are as shown. What is the area of the other paddock?

Answer, page 60

117. Two friends, Alvin and Brendan, played a 25-game tournament of horseshoes one day. They agreed that, to decide the winner of the tournament, instead of counting the number of games each player won, they would count the overall number of points scored.

Alvin started the first game, and after that, the player to throw first was the person who won the previous game. (None of the games were tied.) Over the course of the 25 games, Alvin won six of the games in which he threw first, and Brendan won seven of the games in which he threw first.

After 24 games, Alvin and Brendan had each scored the same number of points. Which player won the 25th game and therefore the tournament?

Answer, page 90

118. You are a contestant on a game show on which you have been presented with the following challenge.

You are put in a booth from which you cannot see out, but the audience can see in. There are three identical switches in front of you; there is nothing else in the booth. Two of the switches work clear light bulbs displayed on a stand on the main stage of the studio; the third works a green bulb on the same stand. All of the switches are in the "off" position when you enter the booth.

After you have flipped whichever switches you decide to flip, you will have to leave the booth to see which bulbs are lit. Once you have left the booth, you will not be allowed to reenter it. Your challenge is to determine which switch controls the green bulb, and you have two minutes to do so.

Of course, you could just guess which switch controls the green bulb, which would give you a one in three chance of winning the challenge. But there is a way to be 100 percent certain that you will win. What is it?

Answer, page 62

119. What word, expression, or name is depicted below?

Ms. Paprika
Miss Rosemary
Madame Sage
Mrs. Oregano

Answer, page 82

ANSWERS

116. Label the triangle as shown and let the area of △ADO be P acres and that of △AOE be Q acres:

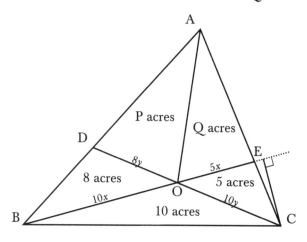

The formula for the area of a triangle is half the base times the perpendicular height. The perpendicular height to C for triangles △OEC and △BEC are the same (both are represented by the line reaching from point C to the extension of line BE), so the lengths of those triangles' bases will be in direct proportion to their areas. Thus if OE is $5x$, then BE is $15x$ and BO is $10x$. Similarly, if DO is $8y$, then DC is $18y$ and OC is $10y$. Using the same technique:

$$\frac{P}{8y} = \frac{Q+5}{10y} \text{ and } \frac{Q}{5x} = \frac{P+8}{10x}$$

Thus $5P = 4Q + 20$ and $2Q = P + 8$, from which $P = 12$ and $Q = 10$. The required answer is $P + Q$, which is 22 acres.

102. All the letters in the series are capital letters without curves. The next term is L.

42. The letters represent the arrangement of men on a chessboard (rook, knight, bishop, queen, king, bishop, knight, rook) in standard chess notation, so the type of music that's missing is Rhythm and Blues (R&B).

10. First, visualize the problem this way:

$$1\ 1\ 1\ 1\ 1\ 1\ 1\ 1\ 1 = 10$$

Between the first two digits, you may or may not place a plus sign. The same choice applies to the second and third digits, the third and fourth, and so on. As long as you place at least one plus sign, you will have a possible solution. For example, here is a way of placing plus signs that is equivalent to $2 + 3 + 1 + 4$:

$$1\ 1 + 1\ 1\ 1 + 1 + 1\ 1\ 1\ 1 = 10$$

There are $2^9 = 512$ ways of placing the plus signs, including the special situation of placing none. Therefore there are $512 - 1 = 511$ equations for the kindergarten to use. As they have wall space for only 500 equations, they cannot show all the solutions.

66.

4	6	3	7	2	6	4
5	5	4	7	2	1	2
1	1	1	7	1	1	1
3	3	5	7	2	3	3
1	4	2	7	2	5	5
6	6	6	7	6	6	6
3	3	3	7	2	5	4
4	4	4	7	2	5	5

81. $111 = 135 - 24$ $666 = (5 \times 4 \div .1 - .2) \div .3$
$222 = 214 + 3 + 5$ $777 = (5 \times 31 + .4) \div .2$
$333 = 345 - 12$ $888 = (15^2 - 3) \times 4$
$444 = (152 - 4) \times 3$ $999 = (5^3 \times 4 \times 2) - 1$
$555 = 542 + 13$

30. Ronald Reagan.

118. Turn two switches on for one minute, then turn one of them off and leave the booth.
- If the green bulb is on, then the switch that is still on is the one that controls the green bulb.
- If the green bulb is off but hot to the touch, then the switch that you just turned off is the one that controls the green bulb.
- If the green bulb is off and cool to the touch, then the switch that controls it is the one that was never turned on.

58.

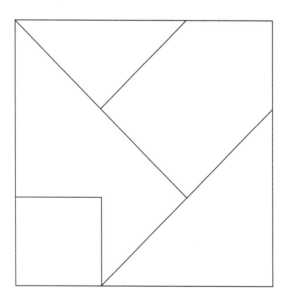

70. The lowest number is 34,217 (equals 102,651 in base eight) and the highest is 250,148 (equals 750,444 in base eight).

99. TED = 682 and VINDICATE = 317,214,568. Thus VIC is $2 \times$ IAN because $314 = 2 \times 157$.

9. The innkeeper of the "Rose & Crown" is talking to a sign painter and is saying "There is too much space between 'Rose' and '&' and '&' and 'Crown.'"

24. 149, 263, and 587.

75. Only five points are needed, as shown in the example below:

	Your hand	Opponent 1	Dummy	Opponent 1
♣	10 9 8 7 5 4 2	A K Q J	—	6 3
♦	—	J 10 9 8	5 4 3 2	A K Q 7 6
♥	—	A J 3 2	10 9 8 7	K Q 6 5 4
♠	A 10 8 6 4 2	K	J 9 7 5 3	Q

Spades are trump. If the defense leads with a diamond or heart, ruff with a low spade and lead the ace of spades. If the defense leads a trump, win with the ace and lead a club for dummy to ruff. If the defense leads a club, ruff in dummy, then lead a trump to your ace.

Continue leading any suit other than spades and cross-ruffing. After the dummy wins the fourth club lead with a ruff, dummy will have no trumps left. You ruff dummy's lead one last time, and then whatever card you lead cannot be beaten.

108. Lemon meringue.

44. Take 9 coins from bag A, 12 from bag B, and 13 from bag C. No coins are taken from bag D. Weigh these coins and calculate the difference between their weight and the weight of 34 genuine coins. Each possible difference can be accounted for with only one pairing of bags (as explained in the table below), making it possible to identify which bags contain counterfeit coins.

In the table below, "A + 2B" indicates that the coins in bag A were overweight or underweight by one gram, and that the coins in bag B were overweight or underweight (whichever is the same as bag A) by two grams. Similarly, "A – B" means that the coins in bag A were overweight or underweight by one gram, and that the coins in bag B were underweight or overweight (whichever is the *opposite* of bag A) by one gram. When D is one of the counterfeit bags, all we know about it is that the coins in it are counterfeit; we don't know whether they are overweight or underweight.

1	B – C	12	B + D	26	2C + D
2	2B – 2C	13	C + D	30	2A + B
3	A – B	14	B – 2C	31	2A + C
4	A – C	15	A – 2B	33	A + 2B
5	2A – C	17	A – 2C	35	A + 2C
6	2A – B or	18	2A + D	37	2B + C
	2A – 2B	21	A + B	38	B + 2C
8	2A – 2C	22	A + C	42	2A + 2B
9	A + D	24	2B + D	44	2A + 2C
11	2B – C	25	B + C	50	2B + 2C

64. There were eight people at the gathering before Vanessa arrived, for a total of 28 handshakes. Vanessa knew seven of the eight other people at the party.

92.

$$\begin{array}{r} 1\,7\,9 \\ \times\ \ 2\,2\,4 \\ \hline 7\,1\,6 \\ 3\,5\,8\ \ \\ 3\,5\,8\ \ \ \ \\ \hline 4\,0\,0\,9\,6 \end{array}$$

110. The contestant should swap the chosen envelope for the other one.

He will only lose the grand prize if he chose it originally. If he chose the wrong envelope (which he has a two-thirds chance of doing), the host will open the other non-winning envelope, leaving the one holding the grand prize. So swapping envelopes gives the contestant a two-thirds chance of winning the grand prize. If you're not convinced this answer is correct, experiment with envelopes of your own and see what happens!

25. The numbers in the column on the left have an odd number of letters, while the numbers in the column on the right have an even number of letters. As "one million" contains an even number of letters, it belongs in the second group.

83.

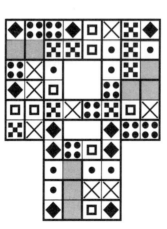

69. Let C be on LB such that $\angle CAL = \angle ABL$.

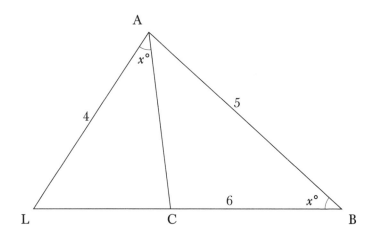

    $\triangle CAL$ is similar to $\triangle ABL$ because:
        $\angle CAL = \angle ABL$ (by construction)
        $\angle CLA = \angle BLA$ (same angle)
        $\angle ACL = \angle BAL$ ($180° - x° - \angle L$)
    The sides opposite angles $\angle ACL$ and $\angle BAL$ are in the ratio 2 to 3, so each side of $\triangle CAL$ is two-thirds of the length of the corresponding side of $\triangle ABL$. Thus $CA = {}^{10}/_3$ and $LC = {}^8/_3$. So $CB = LB - LC = {}^{10}/_3 = CA$, which means $\triangle BCA$ is isosceles and $\angle BAC = \angle ABC = x°$. Thus $\angle A$ is $x° + x° = 2x° =$ twice $\angle B$.

91. The average speed in the first second is 12 inches per second, so assuming constant acceleration, the car's speed at the end of the first second was 24 inches per second. At the end of five seconds, the car would have accelerated to $5 \times 24 = 120$ inches per second for an average speed over the 5 seconds of 60 inches per second. The distance covered in 5 seconds is therefore 300 inches or 25 feet.

14. The numbers on the right are ascending powers of two. The answer to the first equation was given as an example. The rest are: **12** (Angry Men) − **10** (Fingers on a Pair of Gloves) = **2** (Sides to Every Story); **29** (Days in February in a Leap Year) − **25** (Years of Marriage in a Silver Anniversary) = **4** (Suits in a Deck of Cards); **3** (Goals in a Hat Trick) + **5** (Rings on the Olympic Flag) = **8** (Legs on a Spider); **20** (Numbers on a Dartboard) − **4** (Quarts in a Gallon) = **16** (Ounces in a Pound); **18** (Holes on a Golf Course) + **14** (Days in a Fortnight) = **32** (Degrees Fahrenheit at which Water Freezes); **90** (Degrees in a Right Angle) − **26** (Letters of the Alphabet) = **64** (Squares on a Chessboard).

115. Snow blower (S, no W, B lower).

88. Adjacent missiles start the journey $\sqrt{(50^2 + 50^2)}$ = 70.71 miles apart, and by symmetry move at a constant 90° angle to their neighbor. Therefore, with a range of only 70 miles, the missiles will not collide and the fighting unit's base will not be destroyed.

27. The two pieces of land are shaped like so:

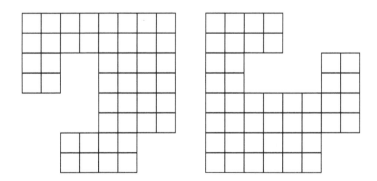

71. Each person consumed eight items, so Tom sold seven items to Harry and Dick sold one. Thus Tom should receive seven coins from Harry and Dick just one.

54. You don't need to know the location of Secret Place to find the treasure. Wherever you stand to follow the instructions, you will end up directly over the treasure. It is buried at a point that can also be found by walking half the distance from Crossbones Rock to Hangman's Tree, turning 90° left, and walking the same distance again.

105. The center of each tree forms a right triangle with the ends of the hedge (as does any point on the curved side). The problem is thus to find an integer less than 1,760 whose square can be expressed as the sum of two nonzero squares in 13 different ways. That integer is 1,105, so the hedge is 1,105 yards long.

Measurements from the first 13 trees to the hedge are (47, 1,104); (105, 1,100); (169, 1,092); (264, 1,073); (272, 1,071); (425, 1,020); (468, 1,001); (520, 975); (561, 952); (576, 943); (663, 884); (700, 855); and (744, 817). The measurements for the other 13 trees are the same, but with the order of the measurements reversed.

1.

$$\left(\sqrt{\tfrac{1}{.1}} + 1\right)! = 24 \qquad 22 + 2 = 24 \qquad 3^3 - 3 = 24$$

$$(4 + \sqrt{4}) \times 4 = 24 \qquad 5! \div (\sqrt{5} \times \sqrt{5}) = 24$$

$$6 \times 6 \times .\overline{6} = 24 \qquad \left(7 - \sqrt{\tfrac{7}{.7}}\right)! = 24$$

$$8 + 8 + 8 = 24 \qquad 9 \times \sqrt{9} - \sqrt{9} = 24$$

Alternate solutions are possible.

11. Two solutions, each using four pourings, are:

	11-cup jug	13-cup jug	17-cup jug
Contents at start	9	9	9
After 1 pour	5	13	9
After 2 pours	0	13	14
After 3 pours	11	2	14
After 4 pours	8	2	17

	11-cup jug	13-cup jug	17-cup jug
Contents at start	9	9	9
After 1 pour	1	9	17
After 2 pours	0	10	17
After 3 pours	11	10	6
After 4 pours	8	13	6

21. $10^5 = 10 \times 10^4 = (1 + 9) \times 10^4 = (1^2 + 3^2) \times 100^2 = 100^2 + 300^2$. There are two other pairs of squares that add up to 100,000 ($12^2 + 316^2$ and $180^2 + 260^2$), but they're not easily found without a computer.

For the second question, we are told that 17 is the only prime factor of 1,419,857. After factoring, we find that $1,419,857 = 17^5$. Proceeding as before, $1,419,857 = (1 + 16) \times 17^4 = (1^2 + 4^2) \times 289^2 = 289^2 + 1,156^2$. (Other, harder-to-find solutions are $404^2 + 1,121^2$ and $799^2 + 884^2$.)

85. The series can be rewritten as $1^2 + 1^3$, $2^2 + 2^3$, $3^2 + 3^3$, $4^2 + 4^3$, $5^2 + 5^3$, and so on. The next term is therefore $6^2 + 6^3$, which equals 252.

37. *Stuart Little.*

28. From the diagram given, construct point A such that AD = CD and ∠ADC is 90°, and extend BD to point E such that DE = BD.

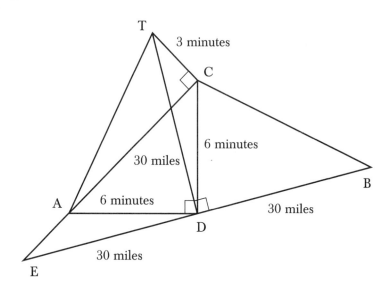

 △CDA is isosceles and ∠CDA is a right angle, so ∠ACD is 45° and ∠ACT = 135° − 45° = 90°.

 AC = $\sqrt{(6^2 + 6^2)}$ = $\sqrt{72}$ minutes of flying time. TA = $\sqrt{(3^2 + 72)}$ = 9 minutes of flying time.

 ∠EDA = ∠TDC (since both are equal to ∠EDC − 90°), so △EDA and △TDC are congruent. By symmetry, BC = TA, and flying the distance BC will take 9 minutes.

78. The letters in NEW DOOR can be rearranged to spell the phrase "ONE WORD."

55. 134,689 = 367².

93. The two solutions are 1,787,109,376 and 8,212,890,625.

45. Since the first player could not determine the color of the ball in box 2, boxes 1 and 3 must have contained red/yellow, yellow/red, or red/red. (If they had contained yellow/yellow, he would have known box 2 contained a red ball.)

If box 3 had contained a yellow ball, the second player would have been able to determine that box 1 contained a red ball. Since he could not do so, box 3 must contain a red ball.

7. The complete division is:

```
            90809
    12) 1089710
        108
          97
          96
          110
          108
            2
```

109. The monks and nuns received more than $56,000 each. If there were five of them, they would receive only $48,000 each, so there must be one, two, three, or four of them, each receiving $240,000, $120,000, $80,000, or $60,000 respectively. Subtracting $56,000 from those amounts gives $184,000, $64,000, $24,000, and $4,000.

Only $24,000 and $4,000 divide evenly into $240,000, so the number of monks and nuns must be three or four. But the number can't be three, since we're told that the monks received the same amount of money as the nuns, so the number must be even. Therefore, there were 60 grandchildren ($240,000 ÷ $4,000), two of whom were monks and two of whom were nuns.

31. Yes; 77 gives the chain $77 \rightarrow 49 \rightarrow 36 \rightarrow 18 \rightarrow$ 8. There is no other two-digit number that requires more than three multiplications.

65. Linda, Marlene, Madeline, Nora. The theme is "women's names."

95. Leaning Tower of Pisa.

22. $138 \times 138 = 19{,}044$.

48. a)

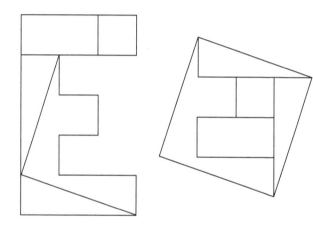

b)

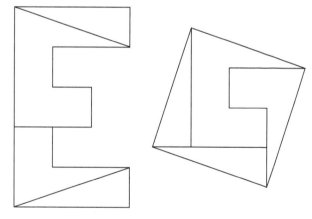

103. If we redraw the circuit as below, the answer is easier to see:

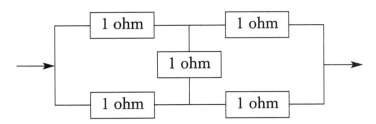

The resistance is $.5 \times 2 = 1$ ohm. The middle resistor has no effect.

86. Raised eyebrows.

39. Label the columns A, B, C, and D from left to right, and the rows 1, 2, 3, and 4 from top to bottom. One solution is as follows:

Move the tile at A1 to the bottom of the column.
Move the tile at A2 to the right end of the row.
Move the tile at A1 to the bottom of the column.
Move the tile at B4 to the left end of the row.
Move the tile at C3 to the top of the column.
Move the tile at A1 to the right end of the row.
Move the tile at D1 to the bottom of the column.
Move the tile at B2 to the right end of the row.

8. The numbers in the series, spelled out, are one, two, four, five, seven, eight, eleven, twelve, thirteen, fourteen, fifteen, and sixteen. Taking these numbers in pairs, each has the same number of letters as the other. The next four numbers are therefore eighteen, nineteen, twenty-one, and twenty-two.

73. Abraham Lincoln.

107. If the first cube had been totally submerged before the second cube was placed on the pond floor, then the second cube would also have raised the water level by three inches. The second cube raised the water level by four inches, so the first cube was not totally submerged before the second cube was placed.

If the first two cubes had been totally submerged before the third cube was placed on the pond floor, then the third cube would have raised the water level by less than four inches. This is the case because it would have taken the submersion of all of cube two *and* part of cube one to raise the water level four inches. Therefore the first and second cubes were not fully submerged when the third cube was placed.

If the three cubes were not fully submerged after the third cube was placed, then the water level would have risen by more than four inches. As the water level did not rise by more than four inches, all three cubes must have been submerged once the third cube was placed on the pond floor.

Let A be the area of the pond's base, s be the length of one of the cube's sides, and x be the depth of the pond before the cubes were added. We then have:

$$3A = s^2(x + 3)$$
$$7A = s^2(x + 7) + s^2(x + 7)$$
$$11A = s^3 + s^3 + s^3$$

Multiplying the first equation by 7 and the second equation by 3, and then dividing each by s^2, we get $7x + 21 = 6x + 42$, hence $x = 21$.

Substituting for x in the first equation, $A = 8s^2$, and substituting for A in the third equation, $s = 11 \times 8 \div 3$, or 29.33 inches.

(For the sake of completeness, $A = 8s^2 = 8 \times 29.33^2$ square inches = 47.8 square feet.)

52. The fifth man received 2,302 coconuts. From the starting pile of 15,621 coconuts, the first man received 4,147 coconuts, the second man 3,522 coconuts, the third man 3,022 coconuts, and the fourth man 2,622 coconuts. The remaining six coconuts went to the monkey.

32.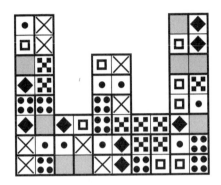

80. $\frac{5}{34} + \frac{7}{68} + \frac{9}{12} = 1$

16.

94. The answer is 111,111,111, and is guessable given this pattern: $11^2 = 121$; $111^2 = 12,321$; $1,111^2 = 1,234,321$; etc.

2. The maximum number of properties owned by Donald is 27 (10 + 9 + 8) and the minimum is 6 (3 + 2 + 1). The number of possibilites for sharing from 6 to 27 properties between three people with no two having the same number of properties is 120.

Since we are told that knowing the total number of properties is insufficient for the daughters to deduce the three inheritances, totals of 6, 7, 26, and 27 can be eliminated immediately. That leaves 116 possibilities.

The eldest daughter is initially unable to deduce the inheritance of her two sisters. This eliminates combinations such as 8/7/5, where the eldest daughter, knowing both the amount of her own inheritance and the total number of properties, could have deduced each of her sister's inheritances. This brings us to 92 possibilities.

Continuing in this vein, after six "no" answers, we have 30 possibilities:

Total	Possible combinations for each total
15	9/5/1, 9/4/2, 8/6/1, 8/5/2, 8/4/3, 7/6/2, 7/5/3
16	10/5/1, 10/4/2, 9/6/1, 9/5/2, 9/4/3, 8/6/2, 8/5/3
17	10/6/1, 10/5/2, 9/7/1, 9/6/2, 9/5/3, 8/7/2, 8/6/3
18	10/6/2, 10/5/3, 9/7/2, 9/6/3, 9/5/4, 8/7/3, 8/6/4
19	10/6/3, 9/7/3

Because the eldest daughter was able to deduce the inheritance of her two sisters at this stage, we can deduce that the total inheritance was 19 properties. To determine whether the distribution was 10/6/3 or 9/7/3, we must look at the eldest daughter's statement that the last two answers (both "no") gave her some information, and see what she would have deduced, knowing that the total inheritance was 19 properties.

	Possibilities remaining
After 4 noes	10/7/2, 10/6/3, 9/8/2, 9/7/3, 9/6/4
After 5 noes	10/7/2, 10/6/3, 9/7/3, 9/6/4
After 6 noes	10/6/3, 9/7/3

Although the fifth "no" helps us (allowing us to eliminate the combination 9/8/2), it would only have provided information to the eldest daughter if she had been told she was inheriting nine properties. Thus the answer is nine properties for the eldest daughter, seven for the middle daughter, and three for the youngest.

62. The numbers used are the first six even numbers. The answer to the first equation was given as an example. The rest are: **4** (Seasons in a Year, Sides on a Square, Faces on Mount Rushmore); **6** (Feet in a Fathom, Pockets on a Pool Table, Characters in Search of an Author); **8** (Arms on an Octopus, King Henrys of England, Pints in a Gallon); **10** (Pins in a Bowling Alley, Years in a Decade, Little Indians); **12** (Inches in a Foot, Signs of the Zodiac, Disciples of Christ or Days of Christmas).

38. H O T
A R E
S E E

101. Although the gravity is lower on the moon than on Earth, a helicopter cannot fly on the moon as it would have no atmosphere to fly in!

46. There is just one, measuring $6 \times 8 \times 10$.

18. $854 = \sqrt{729,316}$.

40. Twenty hexagons and twelve pentagons have $20 \times 6 + 12 \times 5 = 180$ sides between them. Each side is paired with another when sewn, giving 90 pairs of edges to be stitched. The length of thread needed is therefore $90 \times 5 = 450$ inches.

82. $5^3 + 3^3 + 3^3 + 3^3 + 2^3 + 2^3 + 2^3 + 2^3 + 1^3 = 239$
$4^3 + 4^3 + 3^3 + 3^3 + 3^3 + 3^3 + 1^3 + 1^3 + 1^3 = 239$

6.

74. $(1 + 2 - 3 - 4) \times (5 - 6 - 7 - 8 - 9) = 100$. (Other solutions are possible.)

29. The sides of the triangle measure 9, 10, and 17 units.

106. The digits of the code are in alphabetical order. The middle digits are 17.

90. 8π inches, or just over two feet.

34. A domino placed on a chessboard will cover one white square and one black square, so 31 dominoes placed on a chessboard must cover 31 squares of each color. The board described has 30 squares of one color and 32 of the other, so the answer is "no."

57. The terms in the series are 10 in base 10, 20 in base 9, 30 in base 8, and so on. The next term in the series is 70 in base 4, which is 1,012.

19.

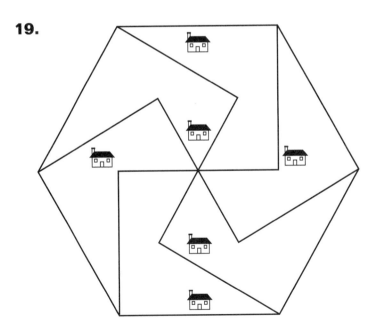

33. Let F be on AD such that CF = CD.

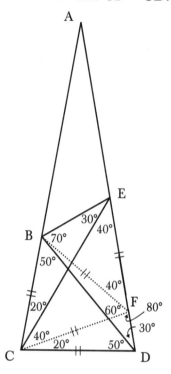

 △FCD is isosceles, so ∠CFD = 80°, ∠FCD = 20°, and ∠ECF = 40° (∠ECD's 60° − ∠FCD's 20°).

 The angles of a triangle total 180°, so ∠CBD = 50° and ∠CED = 40°. ∠CDB = ∠CBD, so △CBD is isosceles and CD = CB.

 Since CF = CD, CF = CB and ∠CBF = ∠CFB = ½(180° − ∠BCF) = 60°. △CBF is therefore equilateral and CB = BF = CF.

 ∠ECF = ∠CEF, so △ECF is isosceles and CF = EF.

 ∠EFB = 40° (180° − ∠CFB's 60° − ∠CFD's 80°). Since BF = CF, BF = EF and △BEF is isosceles, so ∠EBF = ∠BEF = ½(180° − ∠EFB) = 70°.

 Thus ∠BEC = ∠BEF − ∠CEF = 70° − 40° = 30°.

17. From the information about the alternative routes home from the shopping mall, the shopper must live somewhere on the highlighted section or at the circled point in the first diagram below. The information about the position of the cafe then enables both the site of the cafe and the shopper's home to be determined as shown in the second diagram.

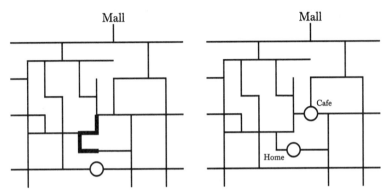

60. The answer is 204 squares. There is one square measuring 8×8, 2^2 squares measuring 7×7, 3^2 squares measuring 6×6, and so on up to 8^2 squares measuring 1×1. This gives a total of $1 + 2^2 + 3^2 + 4^2 + 5^2 + 6^2 + 7^2 + 8^2 = 204$.

113. Here's a lesson in water safety: Susie will not be able to swim back! The current doubled her speed while swimming to the boat, so when swimming against the current, she will make no progress whatsoever.

49. Khaki = arks. The key is to replace each letter with the number that represents its position in the alphabet, and then close up the gaps and respace to make a new word. For example, "beer" is equivalent to "yeah" because beer = 2 5 5 18 = 25518 = 25 5 1 8 = yeah. Hence khaki = 11 8 1 11 9 = 1181119 = 1 18 11 19 = arks.

3. The number 4 is a perfect square.

97. To identify the numbers we are told that we would have to know their product and the smallest number. Since knowledge of the product by itself would not allow us to determine the four numbers, the product must be obtainable in more than one way. A list of such numbers whose factors total less than 18 is given below:

If the smallest number were 1, then knowledge of this fact with knowledge of the product would still not be sufficient to determine the four numbers. Therefore the smallest number cannot be 1 and, by elimination, must be 2. It follows that the product is 120 and the integers are 2, 3, 4, and 5.

Product	1st possibility	2nd possibility	3rd possibility
48	1, 2, 3, 8	1, 2, 4, 6	
60	1, 2, 3, 10	1, 2, 5, 6	1, 3, 4, 5
72	1, 2, 4, 9	1, 3, 4, 6	
80	1, 2, 4, 10	1, 2, 5, 8	
84	1, 2, 6, 7	1, 3, 4, 7	
90	1, 2, 5, 9	1, 3, 5, 6	
96	1, 2, 6, 8	1, 3, 4, 8	
120	1, 3, 5, 8	1, 4, 5, 6	2, 3, 4, 5

53. The sum of the fourth powers of the digits in the number equals the number. For example, $1^4 + 6^4 + 3^4 + 4^4 = 1 + 1{,}296 + 81 + 256 = 1{,}634$.

119. The Spice Girls.

35. One solution is to run a fence from C to B, and another fence from A to E (the midpoint of CD). In the diagram below, Y is the intersection of AE and BC, and X and Z are the feet of the perpendiculars from Y to AB and CD respectively.

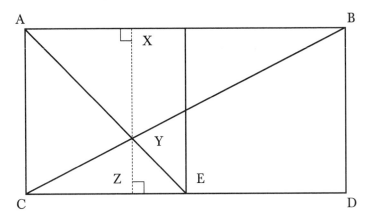

∠CYE = ∠AYB and ∠CEY = ∠BAY, so △CEY and △BAY are similar.

Since AB is twice CE, XY is twice YZ. Therefore YZ = XZ ÷ 3 = AC ÷ 3.

The area of △CEY is ⅓AC × ½CD × ½ = ⅓ × ½ × ½ × (AC × CD) = ⅓ × ½ × ½ × 12 acres = 1 acre.

The area of △ABY is four times that of △CEY (since AB is twice CE and XY is twice YZ) and is therefore 4 acres.

The area of △ACE is one-fourth of ▱ABCD and is therefore 3 acres, so we know that △ACY has an area of 2 acres (since △ACY + △CEY = △ACE, and △CEY = 1 acre and △ACE = 3 acres).

The three areas already accounted for total 7 acres, so the quadrilateral BYED is 5 acres.

Both △ABC and △CBD are 6 acres; the remaining plots up to 11 acres can be found by subtracting the parts mentioned above from the whole.

59. Let Andy begin with B blue socks and G gray socks. Then:

$$\frac{B}{B+G} \times \frac{B-1}{B+G-1} + \frac{G}{B+G} \times \frac{G-1}{B+G-1} = \frac{1}{2}$$

From which $B^2 + G^2 - 2BG - B - G = 0$, so $(B - G)^2 = B + G$. Similarly, let Andy end up with B' blue socks and G' gray socks; then $(B' - G')^2 = B' + G'$.

Since $(B' + G') - (B + G) = 2 \times 24$, we then know that $(B' - G')^2 - (B - G)^2 = 48$. The only pairs of perfect squares that differ by 48 are 1, 49; 16, 64; and 121, 169. The first and third of these solutions are inadmissible because they require an odd number of socks. Therefore Andy started with 16 socks and now has 64.

For the record, Andy started with 3 blue pairs and 5 gray pairs (or the other way around), and thanks to his aunt, now has 14 blue pairs and 18 gray pairs (or the other way around).

13. Thomas started with 251 sugar cubes and made a 6 × 6 × 6 cube, a 3 × 3 × 3 cube, and a 2 × 2 × 2 cube. Once the dog ate one sugar cube, Thomas then made two cubes, each 5 × 5 × 5.

72. A triangle measuring 12 by 16 by 20 will just fit inside a triangle measuring 11 by 60 by 61.

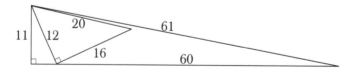

114. $3.16, $1.50, $1.25, and $1.20.

63. 51983.

23. Three planes are needed. The planes set off together and fly one eighth of the way around the world. One then tops the other two up with fuel before returning to base. The other two planes continue until they are a quarter of the way around the world, then one tops up the other with fuel and returns to base. The remaining plane then flies solo until it is three quarters of the way around the world when the above maneuvers are carried out in reverse: one plane meets the first plane at the three-quarter point and gives it a quarter tank of gas; then the two planes fly to the seven-eighths point, where they are met by the third plane, who gives them each another quarter tank of gas. All three planes then use their remaining quarter of a tank to return to base.

76. The integers from 1 to 27 total 378, and in a 3-by-3-by-3 magic cube will appear as nine rows (or columns or pillars). The common sum for this magic cube must therefore be $378 \div 9 = 42$.

Each cell of the top layer of the cube connects to a cell on the bottom layer of the cube via the cell at the center of the cube. These nine lines total $9 \times 42 = 378$. The top layer and bottom layer of the cube both comprise three rows, so between them total $6 \times 42 = 252$. The center cell of the magic cube described in the question must always therefore be $(378 - 252) \div 9 = 14$.

One such magic cube is shown below.

27	11	4
5	25	12
10	6	26

13	9	20
21	14	7
8	19	15

2	22	18
16	3	23
24	17	1

112. There are five ways that Wink can win the best of nine games: 5–0, 5–1, 5–2, 5–3, or 5–4. The respective probabilities of these are: $(1/3)^5$, $(1/3)^5 \times 2/3 \times 5$, $(1/3)^5 \times (2/3)^2 \times 15$, $(1/3)^5 \times (2/3)^3 \times 35$, and $(1/3)^5 \times (2/3)^4 \times 70$. These total 14.5%.

For Wink to win from being down 3–2, he must win three games in a row, or three out of the next four. The probability of this is $(1/3)^3 + (1/3)^3 \times 2/3 \times 3 = 11.1\%$.

Wink should not accept Tiddle's offer. Tiddle could just as well have said, "In nine games, I expect to win 6–3; shall we call it 5–3?" By not accepting Tiddle's offer, Wink risks losing by 5–0 or 5–1, but also leaves more room for luck to work in his favor.

61. Label the five inventors N, O, P, Q, and R, and label their respective inventions as n, o, p, q, and r, where "r" represents the robot. The table below shows the 13 crossings required.

First bank	Boat		Second bank
NOPQR, nopqr			—
NOPQR, pq	nor	⟶	nor
NOPQR, pqr	⟵	r	no
NOPQR, q	pr	⟶	nopr
NOPQR, qr	⟵	r	nop
QR, qr	NOP	⟶	NOP, nop
NQR, nqr	⟵	Nn	OP, op
NQ, nq	Rr	⟶	OPR, opr
NOQ, noq	⟵	Oo	PR, pr
noq	NOQ	⟶	NOPQR, pr
noqr	⟵	r	NOPQR, p
q	nor	⟶	NOPQR, nopr
qr	⟵	r	NOPQR, nop
—	qr	⟶	NOPQR, nopqr

77. Since the ten digits add up to 45, and each is counted twice when the sums are formed, the average sum must be $2 \times 45 \div 10 = 9$. Clearly every pair cannot add up to 9, so there must be at least two different sums.

If there were only two different sums, then one sum would be under 9 and the other would be over 9. However, consider the circle containing the 9. The numbers in the circles on either side of it must be different, so adding each of them to 9 cannot give the same total. Thus we would have two different sums equal to or greater than the required average of 9, which contradicts the initial assumption. Thus there must be at least three different totals.

The diagram below shows one way in which the ten numbers can be arranged to give just three different totals, in this case 8, 9, and 10.

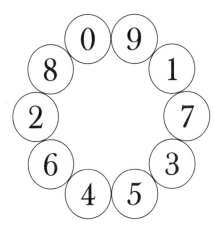

12. Metallica.

41. M, I, and C, spelling "microcosmic."

87. Understudy. The other words contain three consecutive letters of the alphabet; "understudy" has four.

56. The first diagram has one small square in the center; the second diagram has one small square and two large ones. Can you find a second solution?

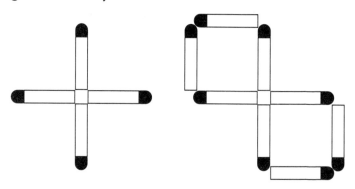

68. $(8 - \sqrt{9})! \times (.9 + \sqrt{.\overline{1}}) = 120 \times .9 + 120 \times .\overline{3} = 108 + 40 = 148$

96. The eight names, from top to bottom, are Nicholas, Jennifer, Geoffrey, Patricia, Benjamin, Samantha, Jonathan, and Rosemary.

47. Breakfast, dinner, tea, supper. The theme is "meals."

111. The question, once the missing vowels (including Y) have been replaced, reads: "What is the lowest whole number that would not be described uniquely if it were written in the same style as this question?" The answer is 8, as "ght" could mean "eight" or "eighty."

26. $2592 = 2^5 \times 9^2$.

79. The divisors of 672 are 1, 2, 3, 4, 6, 7, 8, 12, 14, 16, 21, 24, 28, 32, 42, 48, 56, 84, 96, 112, 168, 224, 336, and 672, which total 2,016, or 3×672.

5. The first sticker Hayley buys will, naturally, not duplicate another sticker she already owns. Buying a second sticker she doesn't already own (we'll call that a "useful sticker" for convenience) will require an average of 250/249 purchases. This is the sum of:

$$1 \times \frac{249}{250} + 2 \times \frac{1}{250} \times \frac{249}{250} + 3 \times \frac{1}{250} \times \frac{1}{250} \times \frac{249}{250} + \ldots$$

The third useful sticker requires an average of 250/248 purchases, and so on. To buy a complete set of 250 stickers this way would therefore cost on average:

$$\left(1 + \frac{250}{249} + \frac{250}{248} + \frac{250}{247} + \ldots + \frac{250}{2} + 250\right) \times 20\text{¢} = \$305.03$$

Using a similar formula, the average cost of buying a complete set of 250 stickers by buying stickers one at a time until getting 225 different stickers, and then buying a pack of the remaining 25 stickers would be $114.24 + $12.50 = $126.74. Obviously that's a better option than buying no packs of 25, but it can still be improved upon. A chart of the expected costs of the different options is shown below:

Packs of 25	1	2	3	4	5
Total cost	$126.74	$105.07	$97.47	$95.66	$97.06
Packs of 25	6	7	8	9	10
Total cost	$100.47	$105.29	$111.13	$117.76	$125.00

Hayley should collect 150 individual stickers before ordering four packs of specified stickers if she wants to minimize her costs.

50. The murder was committed by Mrs. Peacock with a candlestick in the conservatory.

100. Indira Gandhi (in DIRA, G and HI).

117. There were $6 + 7 = 13$ games where the player that threw first went on to win the game. There were therefore $25 - 13 = 12$ games where the player that went first ended up losing the game.

The order of play for the next game changes when a player that went first loses the game. Given that Alvin threw first in the first game and that there were an even number of games (12) where the player that threw first lost the game, it follows that Alvin would have thrown first had there been a 26th game. Alvin must therefore have won the 25th game and the tournament.

84.

3	7	6	2	4	5	1
1	34	4	36	5	30	5
4	6	3	5	7	1	2
5	35	7	32	1	28	4
7	2	1	5	3	4	6
6	28	2	25	2	35	3
2	3	5	1	6	4	7

36.

Basket 1	Basket 2
Weight up	Prince down
Queen down	Prince up
Nothing up	Weight down
King down	Weight and Queen up
Nothing up	Weight down
Prince down	Weight up
Nothing up	Weight down
Queen down	Prince up
Weight up	Prince down

67. Let a, b, and c represent the sides of the triangle. We know that $a^2 + b^2 = c^2$ and $ab = 666,666 \times 2 = 2^2 \times 3^2 \times 7 \times 11 \times 13 \times 37$.

Either a or b is divisible by 37. Since a and b are interchangeable at this point, let's just say that a is the one divisible by 37, and that $a' = a \div 37$. Since $a \geq 666$, then $a' \geq 18$. Since $b \geq 666$ and $ab = 666,666 \times 2$, then $a \leq 2,002$ and $a' \leq 54$.

As a and b (and therefore a' and b) do not share a common factor, possible factors of a' are 4, 7, 9, 11, and 13. Since $18 \leq a' \leq 54$, then $a' = 28, 36, 44,$ or 52 and $a = 1,036, 1,332, 1,628,$ or $1,924$.

By elimination, $a = 1,924$, $b = 693$, and c (the hypotenuse) $= 2,045$.

15. The distances between the six gas stations are 1, 3, 2, 7, 8, and 10 miles.

98. The capital of Norway is Oslo, which is in the word CzechOSLOvakia.

4.

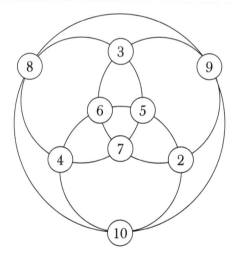

Alternate solutions are possible.

43. In the diagram below, C is the camp, BC is the road across the desert, T is where the traveler begins his journey, and TB is the route due east from the traveler to the road that goes to the camp.

If the direct route TC took 12 units of time to travel, then going from T to C via B would take $5 + {}^{13}/_2 = 11.5$ units of time. The traveler should use the road, then, but where would be the best place to join it?

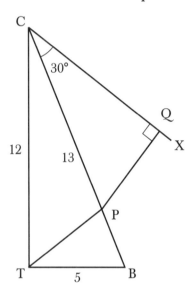

Construct a line CX such that $\angle BCX$ is 30°. Suppose that the traveler goes from T to a random point P on line BC and then, instead of going along the road to C, goes to a point Q on line CX such that $\angle PQC$ is 90°. $PQ = {}^1/_2 PC$ (because the short side of a triangle with angles of 30°, 60°, and 90° degrees is always half the hypotenuse; this can be visualized by imagining an equilateral triangle sliced in half), so the traveler would reach Q at exactly the same time as he would have gotten to C, since it takes twice as long to travel on the desert as on the road.

The traveler's quickest journey to Q would occur when TPQ is a straight line, so he should take the path TP such that $\angle$TPB = 60°, as shown below.

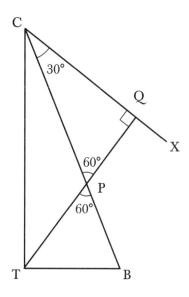

104. The digits a, b, and c are 1, 2, and 7 respectively. $127 = 2^7 - 1$.

20. $12{,}252{,}239 = 2^4 \times 3^2 \times 5 \times 7 \times 11 \times 13 \times 17 - 1$

89. The left side of the equation, $[3 \times (300 + n)]^2$, has the factor 3^2 and so is divisible by nine. Therefore the right side of the equation, $898{,}d04$, must also have nine as a factor. If a number has a factor of nine, then the sum of its digits is also divisible by nine. Hence d must be 7, from which $n = 16$.

51. Wanda uses a rectangular box measuring 36 by 48 inches, which has a diagonal length of 60 inches.

Index

The authors are always pleased to hear of new puzzles. If you have a puzzle that you think we could use in our next book, please send it to us with details on its source and your suggested solution. If we use your puzzle, we will acknowledge your contribution. Our e-mail addresses are timsole@xtra.co.nz and RodM@hotmail.co.uk.

WHAT IS MENSA?

Mensa®
The High IQ Society

Mensa is the international society for people with a high IQ. We have more than 100,000 members in over 40 countries worldwide.

The society's aims are:
• to identify and foster human intelligence for the benefit of humanity;
• to encourage research in the nature, characteristics, and uses of intelligence;
• to provide a stimulating intellectual and social environment for its members.

Anyone with an IQ score in the top two percent of the population is eligible to become a member of Mensa—are you the "one in 50" we've been looking for?

Mensa membership offers an excellent range of benefits:
• Networking and social activities nationally and around the world;
• Special Interest Groups (hundreds of chances to pursue your hobbies and interests—from art to zoology!);
• Monthly International Journal, national magazines, and regional newsletters;
• Local meetings—from game challenges to food and drink;

- National and international weekend gatherings and conferences;
- Intellectually stimulating lectures and seminars;
- Access to the worldwide SIGHT network for travelers and hosts.

For more information about Mensa International:
www.mensa.org
Mensa International
15 The Ivories
6–8 Northampton Street
Islington, London N1 2HY
United Kingdom

For more information about American Mensa:
www.us.mensa.org
Telephone: 1-800-66-MENSA
American Mensa Ltd.
1229 Corporate Drive West
Arlington, TX 76006-6103 USA

For more information about British Mensa (UK and Ireland):
www.mensa.org.uk
Telephone: +44 (0) 1902 772771
E-mail: enquiries@mensa.org.uk
British Mensa Ltd.
St. John's House
St. John's Square
Wolverhampton WV2 4AH
United Kingdom

For more information about Australian Mensa:
www.mensa.org.au
Telephone: +61 1902 260 594
E-mail: info@mensa.org.au
Australian Mensa Inc.
PO Box 212
Darlington WA 6070 Australia